Building Resiliency
*Helping your child build inner-strength
through the adversity of divorce*

By Dr. Lois V. Nightingale

Nightingale Rose Publications
16960 E. Bastanchury Rd., Suite J.
Yorba Linda, Ca. 92886

Building Resiliency
Helping your child build inner-strength
through the adversity of divorce
by Dr. Lois V. Nightingale

A book for divorced parents who want to create a lifetime of inner strength and resiliency skills for their children.

Published by

Nightingale Rose Publications
16960 E. Bastanchury Rd., Suite J.
Yorba Linda, Ca. 92886

Library of Congress Catalog Card Number: 1-5909588791
ISBN ISBN-13: 978-1-889755-08-3
ISBN-10: 1-889755-08-7

Cover Design by Baz Here and Lois Nightingale

Disclaimer
This book is intended to provide information regarding the subject matter covered. It is not designed to take the place of professional counseling. If an adult or a child is having a particularly difficult time handling changes they are facing, seek professional help. If a child or an adult is experiencing signs of depression, severe anxiety reactions, or other psychological disturbances, it is important that to receive professional help. Licensed therapists in your area can be found online under "Psychologists," "Counselors," or "Therapy."

Acknowledgments:
I would like to thank all the families who have shared their stories, concerns, and successes with me, as well as my children, Harry and Teddi, and my sweetheart, Mike, and Laura for all her editing help.

This book is dedicated to all the single parents who work
to create safety and dignity for the chilren they love

Contents

Introduction

Resiliency, the ability to overcome serious hardships, has been researched and shown to be a trait that can be fostered in children. When resiliency is nurtured and developed in children of divorce, it can reduce the negative effects of not only the disruption of the divorce, but it can also increase emotional strength for future disappointments in their lives.

The single most important factor in helping kids develop resiliency, is having at least one stable and connected relationship with a caring parent or caregiver[1]. These relationships (even if there is only one) provide a protection. The caregiver's open responsiveness conveys that the child matters, and that they are seen as competent, even during extremely challenging times.

---

[1] National Scientific Council on the Developing Child (2004). Young Children Develop in an Environment of Relationships: Working Paper No. 1. Retrieved from www. developingchild.harvard.edu.

This special loving parent or grandparent is in a unique position to model and teach adaptive skills. They can give coping strategies for handling difficult emotions and provide positive experiences. These gifts can create strong, resilient and self-confident adults.

Some children have a genetic advantage and propensity for resilience, but even these hereditary factors need to be supported by a positive relationship with at least one caring and connected care giver[2] . This book provides ways to enhance a child's strengths and foster experiences that lead to better coping skills for life.

The longer a challenging circumstance goes on, the more essential the caring parent is in helping the child build resiliency.

Research indicates three factors are supportive of children in building resiliency: 1. A warm supportive connection with a parent or other care giver. 2. Feeling a sense of some control in their lives 3. having opportunities to develop self-soothing skills and adaptive behaviors by the integration of faith, hope or cultural traditions.

This book is a guide for parents to become the supportive, centered and encouraging care-givers that have been shown in research to facilitate resiliency in children who are facing adversity. I have also included resiliency building strategies that parents can hand down to their children so they will have coping skills throughout their lives.

You are never too old to develop strategies for resiliency. Healthy physical activity, positive feelings and self-

---

[2] National Scientific Council on the Developing Child (2010). Early Experiences Can Alter Gene Expression and Affect Long-Term Development: Working Paper No. 10. Retrieved from www.developingchild.harvard.edu.

regulation are great skills for yourself and also to pass along to your child.

It's no secret that no one has ever had a perfect childhood. Of course, some are better than others, but no one breezes through childhood without mishap or disappointment. Families since the beginning of time have faced financial upset and scarcity. Families have faced pressures from extended relatives and society. Families have faced limitations from physical or mental health issues. Families have faced unfair and unexpected losses, betrayals and addictions. Some families have defined themselves as victims of these unexpected detours, while others, saw themselves as tough and strong, specifically because of these unfortunate events and how they dealt with them. They intentionally saw the major disappointments as the fire that tempered their resiliency.

COUPLES HAVEN'T ALWAYS LIVED UNDER ONE ROOF

Married parents haven't always lived together either. Over the centuries, military deployment, staggered immigration, jobs that required extended time away from home, even political incarcerations, have kept children from having constant access to both parents. Famous and influential adults throughout the ages were sometimes raised in monasteries, boarding schools, or moved to different royal residencies every season. These separating situations may not have been ideal, but children in these situations often became more independent and gained a greater sense of purpose than their peers.

Plato was raised by his mother and stepfather. The Dalai Lama was raised in a temple environment after being given over by his parents.

Even successful, empowered adults have not always been raised by their parents. Oprah Winfrey, Jack Nicholson, Barack Obama, Al Pacino, Jamie Foxx, Willie Nelson, Carol Burnett, Maya Angelou, and Eric Clapton, were all raised by grandparents.

Aristotle, Eleanor Roosevelt, Babe Ruth, Edgar Allen Poe, J. R. R. Tolkien, Ray Charles, Ella Fitzgerald, Johann Sabastian Bach, John Keats, Jim Thorpe, L. L. Bean, went on to create powerful lives and impacted millions of others after they were left orphaned at various ages in their childhoods.

We all would like Norman Rockwell picture-perfect childhoods for our children. But even in the worst circumstances, it is possible for children to grow up and be successful, strong and productive adults. Resiliency is one important factor that makes a difference.

SAFETY

Most children today, from divorced *or* intact families, don't face the stressful life and death threats of the past. Children don't have high infant mortality rates, most don't have to drop out of school to work to help provide for the family, and don't have to learn another language or the customs of a new country to survive. Most of our kids have clean water, facilities for bathing and cleaning, climate control, and more choices in food and entertainment than any previous generation. They can have their questions answered in seconds; they have more access to information, academic help, and career options than their ancestors. Remembering that your child is safer than any previous time in history can help you stay focused on the big picture. Even if you're in the middle of a vicious custody battle, try to remember all the ways your child is safe and privileged.

Emotional safety will be discussed later in more detail, but providing this type of safety for your child is something you can give your child every time they're with you. Feeling safe enhances skills of resiliency.

MANY KIDS ARE HAVING A TOUGHER TIME

Unfortunately, kids living in one household or two are also suffering from more anxiety, depression, feelings of alienation and purposelessness than ever before. (The Price of Privilege: How Parental Pressure and Material Advantage Are Creating a Generation of Disconnected and Unhappy Kids. Paperback – July 29, 2008, by Madeline Levine Ph.D.).

However, there are many things a parent, especially a single parent, can do to protect children from these trends.

WHAT'S RESILIENCY?

Resiliency is the strength and flexibility to get through difficult times and come out the other side even stronger.

Forty-five years ago, researchers from Stanford and Cornell University conducted a much-repeated study with preschoolers. They found that one fifteen-minute test with a marshmallow could predict behavior a decade later when the kids were adolescents and adults.

Here's how it went: A researcher placed a large marshmallow in front of the child and told them they could eat it whenever they liked, but if they waited fifteen minutes to eat it, they could have a second one.

The kids that waited and demonstrated delayed gratification to earn the second treat, used many creative strategies to cope with their frustration. Some covered the marshmallow with a tented book; others went somewhere in the room where they couldn't see the temptation. Some kids gave themselves pep talks, and some sang songs to distract themselves.

Waiting for a fluffy corn syrup treat may seem silly and simple, but the results were the complete opposite. The children who were able to wait and earn the second marshmallow had higher SAT scores, lower incidences of addiction and obesity, better reactions to life-stress, better social skills and better scores in a range of other measures of dealing with life. The kids that found coping skills for their frustration, and found the ability to delay having what they wanted, did better in many areas of adult life. These studies have been repeated many times in numerous countries, and the results continue to support and expand on the original findings. Helping your child develop coping skills for frustration and delayed gratification may be one of the most important jobs you do as a parent.

BUMPY ROADS

There are many potential obstacles in childhood: illness, accidents, disability, sibling rivalry, inappropriate relatives, bullying, peer issues after a move, and all types of fears and disappointments. But I find divorcing parents have a unique terror of permanently damaging their children with the trauma of divorce. Somehow the upheaval of divorce seems more volitional or avoidable. In my 35 years practicing as a therapist, I have never seen the path of divorce be "the easy way out." It's a complicated, messy event and everyone in the family feels the pain. But just like any other tragedy a child may face, learning coping skills to live in a divorced family can build self-confidence and resiliency.

UNIQUE LESSONS

I encourage parents to handle the fallout from a divorce the same way they would address any other devastating event that might disrupt their vision of a perfect childhood.

- Teach your child what they can count on during challenging times.
- Model how to trust oneself when the future is unsure.
- Demonstrate how to take personal responsibility for your uncomfortable feelings.
- Exhibit the ways you self-nurture by exercising, eating healthy, having good sleep habits, spending time with positive friends, developing hobbies and expressing gratitude for your life.
- Take your children with you when you volunteer and give back to your community.
- Let them watch you make plans and follow through, no matter what the other parent is doing.
- Talk to them about how you expand your knowledge by reading and attending enlightening events.
- Talk about your feelings, but never make them anyone else's responsibility but your own.
- Share the ways you are responsible for your feelings by participating in a sport, creative outlets, journaling, seeking therapy or joining a divorce recovery group.
- Let your children see resiliency in action. Remember kids do what we do, not as we say.

Chapter One

"When your mom gets home, she'll deal with your detention,"
Chad's father yelled, as the teen turned his back and walked
away.

The tension had been building in their home. The home he
loved with the yard they had landscaped together. The new
granite countertops, the brass leaf-shaped cupboard pulls,
they'd ordered online together after the kids had gone to
bed. Now Chad and his sloppy jeans, was not just missing
homework assignments, he was failing Language Arts all
together.

"You're a liar!" Chad said, slamming his bedroom door.

"You can't talk to me like that, young man!" His father
stormed toward the closed door. He paused and then opened
it. A guitar pick lay on the only part of the floor not covered
by dirty clothes. Military men blew each other up over on
the screensaver on his laptop. School papers poured out of
a black backpack in the corner. Old sneakers and oily fast

food containers were his room's signature smell. "Son, I know you're mad. We're all spinning a bit—"

"She's going to Grandma's," Chad said, in a singsong tone. "I heard you fighting yesterday. She's never coming back here!"

Chad's dad cleared off a chair that used to face the desk, and took a seat. "You're right. It's all up in the air. We're not sure who's going to live where."

"I hate it when you think I'm an idiot!" Chad flopped on his bed and faced the wall.

His phone blared a screaming song every time a friend texted. They both wondered if Chad's mom was one of the musical bursts.

"I never think you're an idiot," his dad said. "You're very aware and observant. I just haven't had the words to tell you."

"But you expect me to tell you the truth!"

"I promise I'll tell you all the facts just as soon as we figure them out."

Chad rolled over and grabbed his phone. He tapped at the screen. "So why are you guys splitting up?" Chad kept staring at his phone. The late afternoon light through the window outlined the fine hair on his chin.

"We've decided we can't live together under one roof," Chad's dad said. It took all his willpower to swallow the real reason, the adult reason- the reason he'd told his friends, but he reminded himself that it wasn't Chad's marriage. It was Chad's parents' divorce, the two people he identified with and looked up to. He reminded himself that Chad was not his friend, not his emotional support. He took a deep breath. "We think we'll be more civil if your mother and I are living *apart," his dad said, "but we'll both be here for you."*

Be Truthful and also Protective

Parents set precedents during times of crisis. If you lie or deny the truth to your child during a divorce, you may be indirectly instructing them to hide their later adolescent mishaps from you. If lying to make oneself look good is the unspoken rule in your household, children will follow suit when they experience things that are hard for them to talk about. Being open and honest, revealing only what a child can handle, is a difficult task.

Telling the truth to kids does not mean sharing with them everything you would say to your friends or to adult family members. Children not only need to know that you won't lie to them, but they need to trust that you will remain the adult and protect them from issues that aren't age-appropriate. Many adult concerns and topics place undue stress on children and distract them from the concerns they should be focused on, like homework and healthy peer relationships.

What NOT to Say

- *"No, we're never going to get divorced."*
- *"Mom's just away on business, she'll be back."*
- *"Dad's visiting his family for a little while."*
- *"There's nothing to worry about"* are lies that will lead to a child's mistrust.

What to Say

- *"I'm not sure what we're going to do, we're taking a time out right now."*

16

- *"We're having a hard time living together, so I'm moving out."*
- *"I know it's confusing. We're a bit confused too, but wherever you are there will always be someone to love you and take care of you."*
- *"I care about your questions, and I'll answer them the best I can."* These are all honest answers, said in ways that are suitable for a child to hear.

DON'T ASSUME YOU KNOW WHAT THEY'RE REALLY ASKING

Children may or may not ask a lot questions. Most of the questions children ask about divorce don't mean the same thing they would mean if an adult asked them. For instance, "Does the new house have a yard?" asked by an adult might be an inquiry about the affluence of the neighborhood, or a comparison to the home being left. A child asking the same question, may be really asking about being able to take their dog to the new residence. An adult asking, "Who wanted the divorce?" may be trying to figure out whose side to take. A child asking the same question may be revealing terror that one parent will abandon them.

It's a good idea to respond to children's questions with a bit of curiosity before giving an answer. Don't assume they're asking what you think they are asking at first. I've seen far too many parents respond with long answers, defensiveness, or even frustration to children's questions, when a child was really only asking for the reassurance that they were loved and safe.

The details of your adult relationship issues shouldn't be shared with your children. Issues about sex and money are certainly none of a child's business. Concerns about addictions may be shared at an age-appropriate level. There are many 12 step programs such as Ala-teen, Pre-Alateen, and Ala-tot, where children can learn about the disease of addiction and how it can affect a family.

Don't Make Your Child Your Peer

If you share the dirty details about what pulled your marriage apart with your children, you're making them your emotional peers and robbing them of their childhood. It's normal to want to vent about the person who betrayed your trust and shattered your dreams of growing old together, but share your anger and devastation with other adults, a support group or a therapist, never with your children. They can't build a healthy self-esteem if they're focused on which parent is to blame.

How to answer "Why?"

Appropriate (and truthful) answers to "Why are you and mom (dad) getting divorced?" include:

- "We've decided we fight too much when we're together."
- "We can't figure out how to get along living in one house."
- "It has nothing to do with anything you or your siblings did or didn't do."
- "These are adult problems."
- "We see the specific reasons that we're getting divorced differently, but we both will always love you and take care of you."
- "It's very complicated, but I always want to know how you're feeling and what your concerns are. I'm always going to love you."

It may be tempting to defend yourself to a child who quotes the other parent's accusations, but do your best to resist the temptation. If you explain how the other parent isn't telling the truth about you, you're putting your child in the middle and making them choose who's lying to them. Defending yourself may seem "fair" and "justified," but any time a child is put in a position to have to make one parent wrong, they lose out on self-esteem and feeling proud of who they are, coming from the two people they love the most.

DON'T TEAR DOWN YOUR CHILD'S SELF-ESTEEM

A child knows that they have two parents, and that they're part of these two special people. These two special people will never be replaced in a child's life. Kids draw their own identities from these two key authority figures. If one parent is "bad" or "broken," a child learns he/she is half "bad or half "broken."

Tell your child things that are true, but *never* things that put down the other half of their identity. Tell your child honest statements, but make sure they're age-appropriate and vague enough for children to be able to ask about what they are really concerned about. Remember, the ending of a marriage is very complex, and the issues have probably been building for years before the final breaking point. You may not even be aware of all the underlying causes of the break up until many years later, and with much reflection. Stay focused on reassuring your child, not on getting them to take your side against their other parent.

Chapter 2

REASSURE CHILDREN THAT THE DIVORCE IS NOT THEIR FAULT

"I'm sorry, Mom! Really!" Nina said. She burst into sobs.

The spelling word was broken off at the second "t." Her workbook lay open, under the table, sprawled on the floor. Jack's video game dinged and beeped from the family room. The smell of cheese pizza in the oven promised a break in the homework torture. A French fry from last night's dinner lay next to the open third-grade book.

Exasperated, her mom sighed, and took two steps into the living room.

"Mom," Nina said. "Mom?"

Her mom wiped her eyes and came back to the table.

"You just need to focus," her mom said.

Nina put her head in her arms. Her muffled words came out in fits and starts. "It's my fault, huh?"

"What?" her mom said.

"Dad left because you guys were fighting about my ADD."
Her shoulders shook.

Her mom remembered thinking that her parents had divorced
because of her acting out as a teenager. "No, no Honey," her
mother said. "Divorce is never a kid's fault. Ever."

Nina looked up with red eyes.

Her mother stroked her long hair. "Divorce and marriage are
only ever parents' responsibilities. Thank you for asking. That
had to be hard. I hope you will always check in with me if
you're feeling responsible for grown ups' decisions."

It's Not Their Fault

It may seem obvious to the adults involved, but a divorce
is never a child's fault. Children have little control over
their lives. They depend on their parents and caretakers for
everything. They don't have much choice about their daily
lives. This fact makes children very sensitive to anything
that may disappoint or upset the adults who care for them.
When a parent is upset, often the first thing a child thinks
is, "What did I do?" or "What did I forget to do?"

Because this process is natural in children, it's important that
parents remind children that adults are always responsible
for their own feelings. Don't say things like, "You made me
mad" or "You'll make me happy if you…"

If you notice your child trying to take responsibility for
your emotions ("What can I do to make you not sad?"
"What can I do to make you happy?" etc.) make sure you
state clearly and directly "I am sad, but I'm handling it,"

or "Thank you for caring about me, but my feelings will change, and I'll be okay in a little bit." Don't say things that indicate your child is responsible for your decisions or behaviors ("I wouldn't have done that if you'd only...." "See what you made me do?" etc.) Children take what you say literally. Model taking personal responsibility for your own feelings. This is essential for building resiliency in children.

When problems show up in families, children often blame themselves. Kids would prefer to feel guilty rather than feeling helpless. Tell children that the divorce is not their fault. As a parent, you can say this directly, but also take other opportunities to remind children that divorce is always an adult issue. For instance, if your child tells you the parents of a kid at school are getting divorced, recap to your child that the divorce is not their friend's fault. If you're watching a TV show with your child and the topic of divorce is portrayed, use the story to point out that divorce is never a child's fault and that the parents are responsible for their own feelings and desires.

As children get older, their theories of why the divorce might be their fault change. A five-year-old might believe their parents are splitting up because they were mean to a sibling. A ten-year-old might think their parents got divorced because of the stress caused by him/her not doing homework. A teen might believe they caused their parents to fight and decide the marriage wasn't worth the trouble, because of their acting out or defiant behavior. Because this list goes on and on as kids mature, it is good for parents to periodically bring up the topic that children can never cause a divorce. All families have stress. All families face unexpected issues. All families have to find ways of problem-solving. All families do the best they can. And in all families affected by divorce, the decision to divorce is never a child's responsibility or fault.

If your child tends to take responsibility for things beyond his/her control, help them find other ways to feel a sense of power. Volunteering, tutoring, coaching and helping others can show a child that they can have an impact in other areas of life. Feeling like they make a difference builds self-esteem. Children have no impact on major adult decisions. Adults are responsible for their own decisions and emotions. But children can have an impact in many other areas of their lives such as sports, grades, hobbies, music, etc. Help your child find ways to feel like they matter and have a beneficial impact in the lives of others. Resiliency is partly about feeling as though they have an impact and can influence things that matter to them.

RESILIENCY IS ABOUT PERSONAL POWER

Use words that indicate you're taking responsibility for your own emotions.

Don't use words or phrases that portray yourself as a victim (i.e., "They did this to me," "It's their fault," "They made this happen," etc.). When children believe a parent is victimized, they want to protect the parent, rather than feeling protected *by* the parent. This robs a child of the innocence and safety of childhood. A child that "grows up too fast" faces many difficult challenges. Children need the safety and simplicity of childhood for healthy neurological and social development. Children need to play, pretend, and create; not develop anxiety by anticipating danger. Give your child the gift of a playful childhood. Let them know adults are always responsible for their own feelings, decisions and behaviors.

Give children the freedom to live in the moment and obtain developmental skills that are age-appropriate. Anxiety and worrying about being responsible for a parent's emotions rushes a child through essential developmental tasks, with poor results. Children who have focused on making a parent feel better, or who feel guilty for the breakup of the family become codependent adults and gravitate to partners they believe they can save or fix. Codependency is a significant cause of depression and anxiety in adults. Let your child know adults are *always* responsible for their own feelings, decisions, and behaviors.

Model Good Self-Esteem

Give yourself credit out loud for the things you do to feel better. Grieving is a long process, being respectful of grief includes embracing your sadness and using coping skills to work through it and coming out the other side stronger than you were before.

Compliment yourself for actions you take to make the world a better place. Model for your children how you take personal responsibility for your own choices, your emotions, and how you express these feelings to others. Show your child that you are responsible for your own happiness. If you use victim statements, don't be surprised if your child picks them up. Kids mimic adults, but in immature and unpolished ways.

Live in gratitude and awe. Say the things about your life that you want your child to say about their own life. When the waves of grief hit, remember you have tools to ride them out. When unexpected sadness climbs out of some hidden pocket, know that you have skills to address it and not make others responsible for your sorrow.

Children learn resiliency by watching the adults they admire be resilient. Resiliency is not about being stoic and unaffected. Resiliency is acknowledging vulnerable feelings while demonstrating how to be personally responsible for them.

Chapter 3

LISTEN QUIETLY, EVEN WHEN YOUR CHILD IS UPSET

"It's going to be okay," Shelly's dad said. "Don't cry. It's not that bad."

But Shelly only cried more.

"Here, here," her dad coached. "Look, look what I got you." He held out a new tablet. "You can FaceTime me anytime. Don't be so sad.

Joe turned off the TV. "Leave her alone, Dad," he yelled.

"Joe, calm down. This isn't about you." Their father glared through his wire-rim glasses. "You think you know what everyone should do."

Joe only escalated. "You never listen!"

"Joe stop being disrespectful! You're going to be grounded if you don't start showing some respect!"

Shelly tugged on his sleeve. "Dad, Joe's just mad."

"There's no reason to be mad. I wasn't even talking to him. Don't you get mouthy too!" Dad took the tablet and put it back in the box. "If you guys can't show some appreciation, I'm not going out of my way for you."

Joe stood up. "Great, you said we could always talk to you about our feelings. You're a liar!" He went to his room and slammed the door.

"Young man, I'm not a liar! You're grounded!" Dad yelled. "For slamming the door!"

"Dad," Shelly whispered. "It's okay for you to feel scared, and it's okay for Joe to feel mad."

Dad's mouth opened, but he didn't have any words.

"And it's okay for me to feel sad," she said.

"I just want you to be happy," Dad said.

"I know," Shelly said. "But sometimes the shortest way to feeling happy again, is to have someone listen and really understand when you're not so happy."

DON'T PUSH THEM TO "FEEL BETTER NOW"

We don't listen well in our culture. We watch people talk over each other in movies, on talk shows, TV; even newscasters don't wait for the other to take a breath before jumping in with a new idea. We have very few examples of real listening in our adult lives.

To make the issues even more complicated, most adults who work with our children have assigned a strange meaning to the word "listen." If you sit in on your child's classroom, scout meeting, or sports practice, you'll hear the adult in charge say "listen" when they mean "obey" or "comply."

Active listening is a special type of listening that increases the connection between the speaker and listener. Active listening includes getting down to eye level with your child and paraphrasing back what they just said. Rephrasing what you heard doesn't mean trying to fix or change your child's perspective or emotional state. Instead, active listening focuses on conveying that you understand what they're saying and that you get how they're feeling at that moment.

Lead with curiosity and show a real interest in your child. Don't try to fix, educate or teach. Real listening can go a long way toward helping a child feel heard and cared for, it also conveys you believe in their ability to handle strong emotions.

It can be hard to hear your child express emotional pain or watch them struggle with anger or sadness. But If you jump in right away, and try to make them feel better (by comforting, explaining, bribing, etc.) even if you mean well, you may be sending them the opposite message. Messages like: "I don't think you can handle your feelings," "I don't think you can figure this out," "I see you as a victim and in need of rescuing," "I can't handle watching you in pain or experiencing such strong emotions," "Don't show me that you feel bad," "Don't have uncomfortable feelings when you're with me," "Expressing strong feelings during times of transition is a weakness," and "Just act like things don't bother you."

Waiting a little bit, while paying close attention, is more likely to be felt as comforting to a child. Not interrupting or giving quick-fix answers conveys that you see your child as strong and resilient. It shows that you believe that they have the ability to self-reflect and self-soothe. You trust that they'll find the words to share what's going on inside of themselves. Pausing for a few minutes before you attempt to reassure them is a powerful statement.

Make sure when you're listening that you're fully present. Close your phone or tablet, turn off the TV, shut your book. Children rarely share their feelings at convenient times. Parents may need to take a break from some other activity when the opportunity to hear children's concerns shows up.

Not all children need to talk a lot. Some children share their feelings by talking about events and stories. If a parent isn't paying attention, they may miss what a child is trying to say.

One in four children are introverted (some families have more or less). Introverts don't have the same need as extroverts to process everything out loud. An introverted child may feel shamed or belittled if held to an extrovert's standards. If your child is on the introverted side, go for walks with them, spend unhurried time in nature, and don't interrupt. An introvert will often interpret an interruption as disinterest in what they're saying. Many times an introvert will communicate better in writing or texting than verbally face to face. There is nothing wrong with this. In fact, teaching an introverted child that how they connect is acceptable can build self-confidence and give them this resiliency tool for the rest of their life.

Highly Sensitive Children (HSC) often make their best decisions relying on their emotions, and may experience deep feelings during family changes. Even if these traits are significantly different than your own, do your best not to criticize them. Educate yourself so you have a vocabulary to help your HSC express these strong feelings in words. The better vocabulary for emotions a Highly Sensitive Child has, the more tools they will have to cope with their feelings.

It is okay to reassure your child and help them focus on the positive. It isn't okay to use the other parent or other household as contrast. Don't compare households. Focus on what you and your child can do in your own home to help them learn ways to handle feelings.

"Why are you feeling that way?" is not a good question. It is likely to sound like "Explain yourself. Prove you have a right to feel that way." Better questions are: "What happened before that?" or "What ideas do you have to help yourself feel better?"

Don't ask questions than insinuate your child can change other people. "Why don't you just tell them how you feel?" "Are you going to stick up for yourself?" "Just tell them you're not going to go."

None of us can change other people. The divorce itself is proof of that. The only person we can change is ourself. When a parent listens (or reads messages in the case of an introverted child) and indicates that they understand, a child will often find answers on their own. Don't be in a hurry to fix how your child feels. Build in a little space between the time a child shows how they feel and your reassurance and problem-solving. Show that you care, and that you believe they are resilient and smart.

Chapter 4

Let Your Child Know However They Respond Is Okay

"Mom!" Jerry moaned.

"Hurry up! We're going to be late," his mom said. She was in morning mode; her coffee was cold, and pieces of dog kibble lay on the floor.

"But it's not fair, and you don't even care," Jerry said. He was clutching a pillow to his chest. His shoes were untied, and his hair stuck out on the side.

"Okay, okay." Her son didn't look like he wanted her to touch him. Her smile would have to do. She plopped on the couch. They'd just have to be late again. "Tell me."

"It's so not fair. When you guys were together I didn't have to do my own laundry." He slouched lower. "You just don't care anymore. I just---."

"You don't know how hard I work. I do all this for you. You're so ungrateful! How long does it take to do a load of laundry? Really?" Her ears rang with exhaustion. She hated leaving

the breakfast dishes, and the rent was late, again. This wasn't the life she envisioned when Jerry was born. She knew how to soothe him back then.

"Mom can't you ever just listen to me?" Jerry's voice cracked. "I just want to have---."

"You're always complaining! Can't you show a little appreciation?" Her mouth was dry. The thought of cold coffee made her stomach lurch. Maybe she was as disorganized as her ex had said. She rolled the keys around in her hand.

"Mom!"

"If you wanted to wear that shirt again, you could've done a whole load in the time it took you to get ready this morning."

The red stick numbers on the digital clock changed. She'd have to walk him in and sign a tardy slip. Jerry's backpack leaned against the sofa. The key fob on her chain peeked from her sweating palm.

"Mom, just listen for once! You don't---."

"Young man," she shouted. "You're just trying to get out of taking any responsibility around here."

Jerry grabbed his backpack and stomped off to the garage and waited in the car. She wanted to tell him however he was feeling was okay. Mornings were just so hard.

She grabbed her phone out of her purse and texted him. "Sorry, I'm not listening so well right now. I do care how you're feeling. I promise I'll listen to how you're feeling about the added responsibilities and how much you miss my doing things for you. I know all these changes are hard. Let's talk at dinner tonight."

Every child is an individual. No matter how well you know your child, they may still surprise you during times of challenge and change. Children who are hyper-responsible, self-motivated and natural caregivers may amplify these traits, or they may regress and need more nurturing and attention. Children who have always been a bit high-need and required more attention, more help with homework and chores may try to be extra perfect. More likely, they will seem less responsible, more distracted, and will need extra prompting and time to complete tasks (even seemingly simple ones like getting into the car to leave for school).

Children's reactions to hearing about your divorce may also change day to day or week to week. The more you can be fully present and engage with your child where they are each day, the more connected they will feel. Some children will want to talk a lot about how they feel, ask questions about what's going to happen, and reveal what they want and hope will happen in the future. Other kids will be reluctant to chat about the changes in the family. They may try to avoid the topic or change the conversation to something more mundane and safe. Both of these reactions may be normal.

It's important to say positive things about how you and others react to the changes you are facing. If you express judgment about the acceptance or anger of relatives, you may be telling your child how to act. If you say complimentary things about how you are handling your divorce, you are giving your child permission to express a wide range of feelings.

If you don't feel like talking, say so and give a time when you'll be available to discuss what your child wants to talk about. If you're experiencing intense emotions, let your child know you are attending a divorce support group or individual therapy. If you're spending time with supportive friends or carving out extra time just to be alone to rejuvenate, compliment yourself aloud around your kids. Indicate that they will not be responsible for your feelings.

When I see children for therapy in my office I let them lead the conversation with topics they wish to chat about. Sometimes it's an issue with a friend at school, or with a coach, or with homework. Children often talk about their feelings in indirect ways. If you only listen to see if the facts they are telling you are true, or are judging to see if what they are talking about is what you think is their most pressing issue, you may miss the most important things they are trying to tell you.

Spend time with your child doing activities like taking walks, riding bikes or cooking together and leave quiet spaces in the exchanges for them to bring up topics. Let your child set the pace. Let them talk as much or as little as they are comfortable. Let them stop whenever they indicate they want to change the subject or wish to be quiet. The less you pressure your child, the more comfortable they will be discussing difficult topics in the future.

They don't need to have everything sorted out immediately. The meaning of the divorce and a child's feeling about it will change over time. All the many implications and potential changes in the family will dawn on children over time. Be patient, understand that a child is processing a lot of information with an immature perspective. Don't push, let their concerns come out as they are comfortable. Resiliency is built over time with patience.

Temperament plays a large part in how people process changes and loss. If your child is more extroverted they may want to talk a lot, even redundantly, about many aspects of the divorce. If your child is more introverted, they may only ask a couple of questions and appear to be satisfied with this amount of information. If your child is more at ease with texting or other brief forms of writing, use them to communicate. Even if you are less comfortable with digital communication try to keep an open mind. You will have more opportunities to understand what your child's real concerns are and more chances to show you are listening if you exchange information in forms they use with their friends.

Provide art materials for processing emotions like magazines for collages, altered books, or sculptures. (Altered hardbound books are a creative way for your child to journal and express their feelings. Buy a used hardback book and glue every ten or so pages together. Then help your child paint, draw, collage or cut out shadow boxes on each page to express how they felt that day or week. Pinterest and YouTube have many ideas on creating altered books together.)

Be curious but not prodding. Sometimes children don't have the right words to express what's going on with them. Let their art say what they may not be able to articulate.

Don't scold or harass your child if they aren't discussing the topics you think they should be sharing. Don't ask them about routines or discipline at the other household. Anything that might sound like interrogation will shut down their sharing with you, and you'll be viewed as pressuring them to give up dirt on their other parent to be used against the other parent. Most children will shut down if pushed to "tell" on a parent.

Handle your own stress. Build in extra time between

activities, so you are not rushed to get to scheduled appointments and school. At the end of the days when your child is with you, eat meals together without the television, computer or cell phones. Take turns going around the table saying what good things happened that day and what you each were proud of. If your child is hesitant, give them an opportunity and then let them know they can change their mind if they wish.

Don't compare how much or how little your child is talking about their feelings or reactions to the divorce with how you imagine they should be talking or how your friend's child is talking to them. Your child is unique. Their response will be their own. Don't put expectations on them. Don't give them the message that you're disappointed with how they show their feelings. Let them be children and don't pressure them into being more mature than they feel comfortable being.

If you're afraid that your child is too emotional and distracted from homework and peer relationships, or is too closed-up and may be depressed, have them evaluated by a professional. Don't jump to conclusions. Don't assume any one particular exchange is the last one you'll have on a particular topic. You'll have many chances over the years to revisit unresolved concerns your child may have.

Remember, setting the tone that you're available and that you care, is more important than having perfect answers for every question and resolving every uncomfortable feeling. This is taking on the role of that important caregiver who helps build resiliency.

Chapter 5

It's Normal for Children to Want Their Parents to Get Back Together

Bill opened the Lincoln Junior High handout. His daughter Sheila's name was listed under the seventh-grade flutists. School performances never start on time, he thought, and took a deep breath. Elliot swung his feet thumping the metal legs of his chair. Bill put his hand on Elliott's knee.

"Oh, leave him alone," Peggy snapped.

Now that he'd moved out, Bill was less than enthusiastic about sitting together. It felt like she was trying to pretend for the other parents. Caring about what everyone else thought, was part of what he'd escaped.

Elliot leaned against Bill. He slipped a tiny hand into his dad's. The kids on the stage were tuning up. The auditorium was getting warmer. Sweat beaded on Bill's forehead. He glanced down. His son was also holding Peggy's hand, the one missing her wedding band.

The conductor raised his baton. Bill wanted to leave. He resisted by forcing his attention on his daughter and her performance.

After the show, Bill knelt down under a yellow parking lot light, and looked into Elliott's eyes. "Kiddo, I remember wishing my parents would get back together when I was a kid." He blinked back tears. "It's normal for kids to want both their parents under one roof. It seems like it would be a lot easier. I know it's really hard, but it's okay to want things that won't happen. We all feel that way sometimes."

Elliot grabbed his keys. "I'm going to unlock the car," he said.

Bill stood up. Their bodies cast long and short shadows by the amber light overhead. He rubbed Elliot's head. "I'm always here to listen if you want to talk. I love you, kiddo."

One of the hardest things for a parent to hear is a child begging for their parents to reconcile. Some children do this subtly, such as drawing pictures of the family back together, or maneuvering both parents to linger during exchanges, or having them sit together at sporting events. Other children are much more active in perusing their wishes, such as trying to hold both parents' hands at once or pitching arguments about why the family should reunite.

It's normal

The first thing to remember, is that it's very normal for children to want their parents back together again. It's convenient to have the two adults they love the most under one roof. They don't want to see the parents they love sad, angry or lonely. Children are dependent on the adults in their lives. They want to feel safe, and having both parents readily available means feeling safe.

Children look through the eyes of innocence, and they can only see events as they relate to themselves. There is nothing wrong with this. Kids are immature. That's the definition of childhood. Your child wishing you were back together with their other parent is a wish made from their perspective.

Be kind in responding to these wishes. Make sure you indicate that what they want is normal. All children with divorced parents wish that their parents could somehow get back together. Don't give reasons for the divorce that put the other parent down. Don't explain in ways that shame the child's wishes or indicate you expect them to put your comfort ahead of their's.

LET THEM KNOW THEY CAN SHARE THEIR DREAMS WITH YOU

Be accepting and kind. Let your child know that whenever they have wants or wishes they can come to you and discuss them. This does not mean you *accommodate* their wishes and wants. What it means is that you'll help them build self-esteem, and give them words for their internal state. It tells them that you're sensitive to how they feel, and that you can help them identify how they feel and what they want. These are essential elements of resiliency.

If your child feels emotionally safe sharing impossible dreams with you, and it teaches them that you will accept them and not make them responsible for your hurt or shock. Then you've upped the odds of your child sharing other difficult topics in the future. If you scold your child for wanting something that caused you so much pain, they will learn to keep their wishes and hopes to themselves.

Open communication is the most safety you can create for your child.

In accepting that most children want their parents back together again, you are not telling your child that this is going to happen. You can compassionately say, "That's a very normal thing to wish for, but parents don't get back together after divorce. Whenever you are sad or wishing that could happen, I'm always here to talk to."

Making it safe for your child to talk about things that are unlikely to happen, is an important part of building resiliency. Trusting they can strive for lofty goals, believing in themselves, and being able to ride out disappointments with self-confidence are all part of resiliency. These children learn it's okay to dream and reach for the stars. If only very reasonable wishes are entertained and discussed with respect, a child learns to be mediocre and never push beyond what is likely in life.

BE RESPONSIBLE FOR YOUR OWN EMOTIONS

Don't get defensive and try to make your child only wish for things you can give them. Let them see you as strong and accepting things that you cannot change (even their wishes). Stand by your commitments when you give your word. You do not have to bend every time someone is unhappy with your decision, and you don't have to explain yourself all the time trying to make everyone understand. Show your child it is emotionally safe to be unhappy and show real feelings around you.

Handle your own feelings of discomfort when your child asks for something you can't accommodate. Learn to cope with feelings of helplessness. Many of the painful challenges of childhood are unavoidable. It's what a parent says about a child's inner state that matters, not fixing it. Talking with care and concern, praising their courage, and being curious about their feelings and wishes builds self-confidence and resiliency.

Chapter 6

THE BANE OF SIBLING RIVALRY

"He hit me!"

"She's on my side!"

"He is taking all the room!"

"Her stuff's all over!"

"You let her get away with everything!"

"He never gets in trouble!"

"Make her stop!"

"Both you kids knock it off!"

"But---!"

"I mean it!"

"I didn't to do anything!"

"Both of you cut it out!"

At a time when extra energy, creativity, and patience may be at their lowest, sibling rivalry is likely to escalate. One reason is that kid's behavior often follows what parents are modeling. When parents are demonstrating fear, anxiety, competitiveness, defensiveness, and are on the lookout for slights or disrespect, kids will take these as cues for their own behavior.

The more civility and politeness you can manage with your soon-to-be-ex, the better modeling you give your children for the times in life when they're frustrated with someone else's actions.

The underlying motivation for sibling rivalry is competition for parental resources. At a time when finances, leisure time, and individual help may be at premiums, sibling rivalry is likely to increase.

A brother or sister is a great target to try and control when other aspects of life seem chaotic. At times of crisis or change, children may take their anxiety and agitation out on their closest rival. It may be difficult not to take this personally when you need their cooperation the most, but it isn't about you. It's a normal developmental process, which may become amplified at a time of stress, because children often regress when they need more emotional support or psychological reassurance. This regression can wear on a parent when children are acting younger than they did just a short time ago. Regression is nature's way of helping children get the extra nurturance they need during times of stress.

Be kind to yourself. It is difficult to do everything that needs to be done, and some things will get left out or be put on the back burner. The more patience you show, the less sibling rivalry kids will display. Being in a hurry, expressing urgency or anger, will all be interpreted by children as "there's not enough." Slow down. Give yourself extra time. Kids want to feel important to you. Use the transition time between activities to create bonding with each child. Play guessing games in the car. Take turns putting toys away. Sing silly songs during bedtime hygiene routines. While it may seem like the next activity is more important than the transition time in between, the urgency to get somewhere else is interpreted by children as a lack of attention, lack of caring, and a lack of being seen for who they really are. Kids feel loved and safe when parents are in good moods and playful. Show kids how to compartmentalize and be fully present in the activity at hand. This skill will serve them over and over in their lives and provide resiliency.

When kids are fighting, try to address the victim first, not the aggressor. This can be difficult since it's not our first instinct as protective parents, but you don't want to reinforce the aggressor by wining your undivided attention if they attack their sibling. (If you ignore the victim by grabbing the aggressor or walking the aggressor down the hall or spend time lecturing them, the victim is inadvertently getting ignored by you.)

Being a good listener is more important in addressing sibling aggression than explaining or lecturing. Try to get the agitated child to vent to you. Ask them how they feel. Ask about what happened just before the outburst. Ask what they wanted. Don't try to talk them out of their agitation. Don't try to explain to them why they shouldn't be upset. Don't try to give them another perspective. Listen and reflect back what you hear. Pay attention and show compassion. You'll be surprised how much less of their frustration will be taken out on their siblings.

Since sibling rivalry isn't about not liking each other, but
44

rather about competing for parental attention, finding alone time with each child will go a long way. Schedule some individual time every week to spend with each child. This may take some planning when there is only one parent in the home, but even a half hour alone with you will be excitedly anticipated by a child, Looking forward to their special time with you can help create more patience between siblings.

Under the best of circumstances, sibling rivalry is often the most challenging aspect of family life. When a family is in transition, this challenge can seem overwhelming to a parent. As you address your children's rivalry, speak the way you'd like them to speak to each other. If you raise your voice and threaten, they'll try to get each other to comply the same way. Don't scold, lecture, threaten, or be redundant. Model by reflecting back their perspective and being compassionate with their viewpoint.

Though regression and increased sibling rivalry may be exhausting at a time you have little extra to give, try to remember that through your responses you are teaching your children lessons for a lifetime. Active listening, patience with unreasonableness, kindness, slowing down, giving individual attention and how to compromise are all tools they will need for resiliency later.

Chapter 7

"Mommy!" Erin complained. "I'm scared."

It was the same every night that her daughter was at her house. The bedtime routine went well, dinner, baths, teeth brushed, prayers said, an extra drink of water, and then the fears started.

Stacey had no idea what more to do. She'd explained that there were no such things as ghosts, the boogeyman or monsters. She'd bought the princess night light Erin wanted, the one that cost three times more than the simple plastic one. She'd banned any violent TV shows. She'd yelled, scolded, even threatened to take away favorite toys. Nothing worked. The relaxing music on Erin's pink phone was even making her *sleepy.*

It had been another long day. Stacy was exhausted. She bit at a hangnail and tears burned in her eyes.

"Just go to sleep," she snapped.

"But Mommy, there's something in here... REALLY!" Erin wailed. "Pleeease!"

I bet she doesn't act like this at her dad's house, Stacy thought. She'd read an article online about the developmental stages of eight-year-olds. She knew an active imagination was normal and that the night-time fears weren't likely due to the divorce or any real trauma, but more likely due to her daughter's intelligence and creativity. This information reassured her, but she was still exhausted.

"Sweetie, I was scared of things at night, too, when I was your age," she said. "I'm always here for you. Let's come up with some ideas to help you feel safer."

A Hello Kitty hair clip lay on the floor, Erin's purple tee shirt and socks were piled in a heap. The phone continued to play relaxing music. Erin clutched the edge of her comforter.

"I will always protect you," Stacy said. "And you can always tell me when you're afraid."

"Mommy," Erin said. "Will you make the monsters go away?"

Stacy stepped back into the hall and came back with a clear spray bottle. She'd made a label with a monster face and an X over it and filled the bottle with water.

"How about some anti-monster spray?" Stacy said. She handed the bottle to her wide-eyed daughter who began squirting every corner of the room.

"Go away!" she barked. "Bad monster!"

They both laughed, and Stacy kissed Erin good-night.

As mentioned before, children are dependent on the adults in their lives for all their needs. When major changes take place in a child's life, they are understandably afraid. They don't get to have a say about where each parent will live, what school they will end up at, or how money will be spent.

Children at different ages naturally have fears because of developmental processes. Toddlers do not have object permanence and may be afraid when a person or object is out of sight. They don't understand the person or object can reappear. At seven, a child can understand that death is permanent and re-processes past losses with this new information. Around puberty, children understand there is sexual tension and start flirting with romantic relationships. At each age, children are aware of new facets of life.

Your child may have seemed calm and accepting of your separation or divorce when it happened, but may develop fears later. These may not be due to any change in circumstance, but a development stage that a child has entered. As children mature neurologically, they have a greater capacity to understand the dangers and pleasures of the world around them. I encourage parents to read about developmental stages of their children with each birthday. Louise Bates Ames has a series of books, starting with "Your One-Year-Old" and progresses through adolescence. Many parental anxieties can be relieved by staying updated with research and descriptions of the ways children act and react at different ages.

Frightened single parents can mistake new fears, telling lies, back talking, daydreaming, peer issues and a slew of other behaviors as indications that there is stress in the other parent's home. In reality, these irritating, but normal behaviors may have nothing to do with either residence but rather a child's age.

It is important to take a child's emotions seriously. Belittling or minimizing a child's feelings creates distance. Dismissing their fears as "ridiculous" or "irrational" will only serve to have your child withdraw from you emotionally and will decrease the chances of them sharing difficult situations and emotions with you.

Most children develop nighttime fears at some point during childhood. Some want to sleep with the light on, others want reassurance, while others want to sleep with a sibling or parent. These nighttime fears may be of monsters, bad people, or fictional villains. Try to remember that while the feared creature may be fantasy, your child's feelings are very real. They're scared, feeling helpless and vulnerable. Interact with them in respectful ways, being kind about the fears they are experiencing.

The calmer you are, the more you are demonstrating to your child that you feel safe and that you are not afraid of the danger they are crying about. If you escalate and yell at them, your child will be more anxious. No child wants a parent mad at them. Try to stay calm and problem solve with your child. Sometimes just reassuring them that you are nearby is enough. Other children want to have some tangible way to feel safe. Creating an alarm with pie tins and string can be a way of showing you understand that they are afraid.

Often children do not have words for what they are really worried about. It could be that a peer at school made fun of them, or that they are afraid the teacher will call on them and they won't know the answer. They may be afraid that they will have to change residences again or that they are really the cause of the divorce.

While there are many uncomfortable things you cannot change in your child's world, you can let them know it's safe to tell you about their fears. Reflective listening and being fully present when they talk to you conveys that they are okay and still lovable, even when they're scared. Help build resiliency by showing compassion when your child is frightened, especially about topics over which you have no control.

Chapter 8

Ask Your Child About Friends Whose Parents are Divorced

The kids left the dishes on the counter again.

Carol emptied the dishwasher. The kids had to see how much more she had to do now. They had to get it. Everything was behind: the dishes, the laundry, the bills, even the oil change.

"Hurry up! We'll be late," she called.

Backpacks and untied shoes flapped to the car. Carol wasn't sure how long it was safe to drive after the service light came on. It was the least of her worries right now.

"You didn't sign my..." Matt said, from the backseat.

"We haven't talked about it, yet," Carol said.

"I can't go back to school until you do." Matt flopped back against the seat.

"Well, all right, but we'll talk about it tonight. You can't keep

distracting other students."

"You always think it's my fault!" Matt said.

"Matthew is a bully! Matthew is a bully!" Catrina sang.

"Kids, that's enough," Carol said and turned up the radio.

The texting driver made them miss the left turn.

"Owe!" Catrina screamed.

Electricity shot through Carol. "Stop it, you two!" she yelled.

She was always on Mother Bear alert these days. Danger was everywhere, and she couldn't protect them.

That evening she took dinner out of the bags and put it on real plates with napkins. Pretend it's not fast food, she thought.

She turned off the TV to howls of protest.

"We need to talk," she said.

"After this show."

"This is the good part."

"How about during the commercial?"

"Talk to Matt. I didn't get in trouble!"

Carol tapped the butter knife she cut the burgers with against a glass.

"Ding dong, the witch is dead," Matt made a hanging gesture.

Catrina stuck out her tongue.

"Kids!" Carroll said.

"M—um!" Matt complained. "We know, we can always tell
52

you how we're feeling," he mimicked in a sing-song voice.

Carol felt her face flush. "No," she said. "I wanted to know about the kids in that show."

"The one we had to turn off at the good part?" Catrina whined.

"Yeah," Carol said. "What do you think of the parents?"

Matt was chomping on a fistful of fries.

Catrina jumped at the chance to outshine her brother. "He's like Vicky's dad."

"Oh really?" Carol asked. "How?"

Matt slurped his soda. His black hair stuck out on one side. The paper wrapper from his straw had missed the trash can.

"He lives with a different family," Catlin said.

"New one," Matt interrupted.

Carol's phone played morongas from the kitchen. She ignored it.

"How do the kids feel about that?" Carol asked.

"Ma-um," Matt rolled his eyes. "Really?"

"Yes," Carol smiled. "I want to know."

"Then you should have let us watch the good part," he said.

"What do you think was going to happen?" Carol asked.

"A.J. was going to have to go save his dad from the sinkhole in the backyard."

"Do you think he'd save his dad?"

53

"Sadie had to save her dad once," Catlin said.

Carol looked surprised. "Really? From what?"

"Sadie's dad says she's a 'lifesaver' when she helps him bring in the groceries."

One of the biggest mistakes I see parents make when they speak to their children about divorce is forgetting that children are often afraid of saying something wrong or making parents upset.

Asking direct questions like, "How do you feel about us getting divorced?" "Do you have any questions?" "What are your concerns?" "What do you think about us getting divorced?" may elicit answers in some children, but most kids will withdraw and feel pressured to come up with the "right" answer, the answer that will please their parent.

It is easier to start a conversation about feelings and possible fears by asking about their friends' families that are divorced. Asking kids about another family or other kids lets them off the hook from feeling like they might have a wrong answer or that they have to be too vulnerable.

A child is more likely to talk about fears that the police will have to come, that one parent will move far away, or that a parent's new partner is going to move in right away, if they can address these fears by telling stories about a friend or TV show.

When I work with young children in my office, I have them create a sand tray picture of their family doing something. I have several boxes filled with small toys (people, animals, trees, marbles, cars, rocks, home furnishings, etc.) One box is half-filled with fine sand and children stand the toy figures up in the sand to create pictures. Kids are more likely to share their feelings during play and are more willing to act out or demonstrate their inner thoughts and feelings with toy figures. This provides a safe, "once removed" way for them to convey fears or events they might not have words for.

Providing drawing materials, costumes to put on "shows," telling back and forth make-believe stories where you take turns adding lines to the plot, or even drawing chalk pictures on the patio are all likely to provide more self-revealing information than direct inquiry.

It is probable that your child has received most of their ideas about divorce from friends and TV. Asking about how their friends feel about being from divorced homes, or with parents that live apart, gives your child the chance to tell you unfortunate events that they may have heard about divorce. While what has happened down the block or on TV may have almost nothing in common with your divorce, these stories can give you information about your child's fears and expectations around divorcing families.

When you watch TV or movies together, and the subject of divorce is portrayed, take the opportunity to be curious about what your child thinks is happening or what will happen to the children in the story. Don't be discouraged if your child is one of those kids who doesn't talk much about feelings. Take your clues from what they say about other families who've faced divorce.

When discussing divorced families that your child knows, make sure to address emotions and hopes, not just specific facts. While it may be interesting that Billy's father drove off in the middle of the night with no shoes, asking your child how he thinks Billy felt that night, and what your child thinks Billy wanted to happen next, can be of even more interest. Children are concrete by nature, and may have difficulty expressing abstractions, such as feelings and wishes. Listen to their stories, don't try to figure out if they are accurate or not. Listen for the emotional truth, focusing on their internal states. What feelings are they trying to tell you? What wishes or fears are they trying to express? Validate feelings and hopes, even if there is nothing you can do to change the circumstance. You can always indicate to your child that you really "see" them and really understand how they are feeling.

Even if you are not sure your child's story about another divorced family is perfectly accurate, listen for their emotions, their fears, and where they may be indirectly asking for reassurance. This may be the only way your child feels safe enough, or has the words to talk about your divorce. Don't address the veracity of their story. Be patient with half-truths or outright lies that children tell at this time. Try to look past the facts of the story and inquire about the feelings and hopes they have, as if the story were true. You can talk about telling the truth and how lying affects how others see your child at a later date. Now is the time to gather all the information you can about what your child's experience and fears may be. Staying connected to, and aware of, their feeilngs and hopes is essential for healthy resiliency.

Chapter 9

Don't Put Your Child in the Middle or Try to Make Them Take Sides

"Mom says you spent my money for college!" Danny yelled. "All you ever think of is yourself! I hate you!"

Ron took a deep breath. Every cell of his body wanted to scream that it was a lie. How dare she tell Danny those terrible things! The court order stated they weren't allowed to talk negatively about each other to their son, or even if he was nearby or within earshot. This was parent alienation. He needed to explain how wrong this was.

Ron stared over Danny's shoulder and out the living room window. The rain outside matched his mood.

"Danny," Ron said. "It's not---"

"Dad," Danny said. "I don't want to hear whatever you're going to say."

"Don't be disrespectful. I just want to explain---"

Ron's head was spinning. He didn't want to make his son take sides, but it was unbearable that his son thought something about him that wasn't true. The book his therapist recommended was on the coffee table. He'd gotten through more than half of it. He'd made a commitment that he wouldn't defend himself to his son. The therapist had reassured him that his son would understand his mother's issues by the time he was an adult He longed for more simple times.

"Son," Ron started again. "How did you feel when you heard that?"

"Are giving me that psychobabble crap?"

"Danny," Ron sat down. "I do want to know." Ron ran his hand through his hair. "I know this is hard. I can't even imagine. I know you're having to grow up faster."

Danny plopped down on the couch too. Tears welled in his blue eyes. His freckled face flushed and his knee bounced. He rubbed his sweating hands on the legs of his jeans. "I know, Dad," he said. "I just hate it when Mom complains about you. I just wish everyone could get along, or at least leave me out of it."

Before attending therapy, Ron thought triangulation, and making a child take sides, only meant giving his son messages to carry back and forth, or asking his son where he wanted to be on holidays. He was surprised that "putting him in the middle" also included sticking up for himself against gossip from the other side. Ron put his arm around his son, who was almost as big as he was.

"I'm always here for you. I hope if you feel like it, you'll also tell me how you feel." Ron gave his son a hug.

"Yeah Dad," Danny said. "Sure."

Every parent who has learned about the dos and don'ts of divorce knows they're not supposed to put the child in the middle or make them a "pawn" in the battle of divorce. The challenge is being able to spot the triangulation when you're doing it. It's so easy to see when the other parent is using the child for their gain, or emotional welfare, but it can be nearly impossible to see when we're doing it ourselves.

The primary reason for this is that most parents are not trying to put their children in the middle or make them take sides, they are just trying to survive the loss of a spouse, extended family and a social network that was contingent on being a couple. With all this loss of connection, it can be terrifying that a parent will also lose the emotional bond with their child. This fear often leads parents to say and do things that they would otherwise never think of doing or saying.

When a parent is fearful that their community or the extended family will judge or blame them for the divorce, they may be extra sensitive and defensive. They may interpret a child's desire to comfort and protect their other parent as betrayal or criticism.

As parents struggle with their own new identities, it may be far more difficult to view their children as opinionated individuals seeing the world through their own eyes. All parents tend to think that their children are growing and maturing more slowly than they really are. Part of this is because just as parents are developing coping skills for one developmental stage, the child is blooming into a new one that requires different discipline skills, different communication skills, and different motivational tools. Add the need for more vigilance as to what behaviors a child may pick up from their modeling, remember all of this can be overwhelming in the best of intact families.

When a parent doesn't see a child for days at a time, these developmental stages can be almost impossible to monitor.

The most important thing to remember in speaking with your child, or within earshot of your child, is that they are pulling their identity from both parents. If they come to believe one parent is "bad," "mean," "stingy," "weak-willed," "a liar," "a cheater" or "unreliable," then a child will believe this is true for fifty percent of themselves. The best thing you can do for your child's self-esteem during a divorce is to never belittle or demean their other parent when your child can hear you.

"But I never say anything bad about their other parent," I often hear a parent protest, as they continually defend themselves against what they've heard or they believe that the other parent is saying about them. This is triangulation. It makes the child take sides and have to decide who is telling the truth and who is lying. It's a horrible position for a child to be put in.

When faced with an accusation you know is not true, try to put your child's feelings first. If you defend and explain yourself and give facts proving the other parent is a liar, you are demonstrating that your feelings matter most and that how your child perceives you is more important than letting them know that you're there for them.

A good way to begin a conversation where every cell of your body wants to be defensive is to say "Really? And how did you feel when you heard that?" Beginning with curiosity about your child's feelings and emotions indicates that you care more about them than how you are perceived. It demonstrates that you are strong, can take it, and that you will always care about how they are doing before worrying about yourself. It shows that whatever the mistruth was, it was so insignificant and ridiculous that it didn't even warrant your defense. (In reality, we are only defensive about things we are afraid are a little bit true. Think about a time your child was extra defensive. What did that mean to you?)

It can be emotionally excruciating for a parent to hear gossip, especially if it's untrue or embarrassing, carried home by one's child. The shock and rage can be hard to contain, so this is a good time to take a break from the conversation and calm the adrenalin in your body before you speak. Only reply to a comment when you feel sure you can respond calmly and put your child's needs ahead of yours (your need to be seen accurately, your need to defend yourself, your need to have your child see you correctly, your need for retaliation, etc.).

You are your child's protection and safety. If they have to worry about how upset you are, they won't be able to tell you how they're handling the information, whether it's true or not. Over the course of their childhood, the truth will be revealed. Not by you, but by their own observations or others. Trust that if you stay centered and don't lower yourself to the level of gossip and belittling of your child's other parent, you will be seen as the stronger, more powerful parent that can handle your own feelings. Demonstrate to your child how to not lower themselves to the level of peers who say means things about them and/or compete in unjust ways. Model resiliency by waiting for the truth to come out on its own. Don't eat the first marshmallow and lose out on the long-term benefit.

If you find you can't focus on the moment with your child and the truth is burning to get out, start a long letter or journal addressed to your child. Don't give it to them. Hold onto it. When they are 18 or 25, take them out for a nice dinner, and if you still feel the need to explain yourself, give the information to your adult child who will be better able to handle the big picture.

Life isn't fair. Demonstrate dignity, grace and rising above the unfairness for your child. As they build resiliency over the years, they will reach back to what you taught through your actions. You are building a legacy. If you're undecided about what to make a big deal out of, and what you want to rise above, picture your child telling the story of this situation to your grandchild, and then your grandchild telling it to your great-grandchild. Decide if it's worth it to roll around in the mud. You're building resiliency through this as well.

One of the most difficult situations a single parent can face, is when their child speaks to them in a demeaning way, reminiscent of how their ex used to speak to them (or may still speak to them.) Believe it or not, this is also an opportunity to teach a child resiliency skills.

As mentioned previously, children often have difficulty finding the right words to ask about things that they find confusing. Parroting cruel or disrespectful phrases they've heard at the other house hold, is often an indirect request for help. They need help in figuring out how they themselves can respond to these mean statements. Remember, if your ex was mean, and said hurtful things to you when they were upset, they may be saying similar things to your child when they're upset now. You have no ability to change anything about your ex. But you can model strong, emotionally detached and centered ways of responding to bullying and verbal abuse.

Defending yourself, striking back with anger and

disrespect, lecturing, blaming, and one-upping are dangerous communication patterns to model for your child. Teaching them to go toe-to-toe and stick up for themselves, when there is absolutely no hope of them being heard or accommodated, is to inadvertently set them up to be further belittled and shamed at the other household.

Rather than arguing back, or demanding respect, say things like, "I can see you're upset," "You sound really frustrated," "You seem disappointed in what happened," "I'm glad you could tell me this is bothering you," "It seems you don't think I get what you're saying," "It sounds like you think I don't care about how you're feeling," "Thank you for bringing this to my attention," "You sound frustrated," "This isn't how you thought it would go, I'm sorry," " I always want to know when you're disappointed about something," "I got it," "I am annoyed, and my feelings are my own responsibility."

Even if you believe your ex is respectful to your child but says mean things about you to your child, or in earshot of them, you still regain your authority by not lowering yourself to that type of communication. If your child can knock you off balance and get you to participate in disrespectful banter, they can't trust you will protect them. If a child can provoke you into doing the exact things that you tell them not to do (yell, speak disrespectfully, argue, etc.) how can they trust that you will be able to resist the provocation of a full-grown adult?

In order for a child to trust that you are strong and will have the ability to keep them safe, they may poke at you and see how you respond. If they see you remain calm and unruffled, they will build trust in you. And the more you

63

model how to keep your cool when someone, anyone, is disrespectful, the more resiliency you provide for your child.

Show them how to handle verbally combative people by how you respond to them when they're upset and saying hurtful things. Never demand that they change in order to handle your emotions for you. Demonstrate that you are responsible for your own feelings and can stay calm and centered when someone (even them) are upset around you. The strength and resiliency you model will go a long way toward giving these skills to your child.

Chapter 10

"Yes," Barbara sighed. "I'll be fine. You just go have a good time. I'll miss you." She leaned against a post on her porch.

"I love you, Mommy," Ben said. "Don't be so sad. I'll see you soon."

"I'll try. Just remember, you're My Little Man. Give me one more kiss. I'll be waiting here for you." Barbara held her son and kissed the top of his head over and over. "You'll be alright. Just get through the weekend."

Ben pulled away and frowned. "You'll be okay, Mommy. I'll be back soon." Then he ran to the car where his dad was waiting.

Barbara slumped onto the porch swing and wiped her eyes. Mascara smeared on her hand. She felt sad and a little guilty. There was an empty pit in her stomach. A dandelion was growing in the crack in the sidewalk. The silver mailbox at the curb overflowed with ignored mail. Her phone had stopped ringing with social invitations. Emails were mostly forwarded pictures and jokes. She didn't open them anymore. A small Transformers toy lay in the brown grass.

"I'll go bake cookies for when he comes back on Sunday night," she said to herself. She pulled her sweater around her and lumbered back inside.

The phone vibrated on the table. Barbara picked it up and looked at the screen. It was her cousin. They'd once been close. They loved antiquing and finding unique gifts for family birthdays. She picked it up, put it back down, and then picked it up again and swiped the screen.

"Hi Mar," Barbara said.

"I'm in town, Barb," her cousin said. "How about we go on an adventure?"

"Well, I've got a lot to do---" Barbara scooped up the dishes and put them in the sink, phone to her ear.

"What? Ben's at his dad's this weekend, right?"

Barbara paced. "I need to do his laundry and buy groceries for his lunches next week. I'm going to organize his backpack so he can---"

"Barb, you need a life. I'm coming to get you. We're going to dinner, and we'll figure out which shops we're going to---"

"But Ben needs---"

"Ben needs you to have things to look forward to with people your age." Barbara held the cell phone away from her ear and scowled at it.

"Sure. Fine. Come on. We'll go get a bite to eat." She knew her cousin was right. She just hadn't known where to start.

There is so much to do as a divorce unfolds. There is never enough time and never enough money. You will feel pulled from many directions and fear that you aren't being competent at any of them. It will seem like a luxury to spend time with your friends. The truth is that connecting with the people who care about you, will cheer you on, and give you a shoulder to cry on is crucial to having enough energy to parent well through this difficult time.

If you find you have a short fuse and small things send you through the roof, you might need more time with your support network. If your support system was your in-laws or couples who you don't feel comfortable with right now, then you may need to focus on making a new friend or two, join a MeetUp.com activity, or sign up for a divorce recovery group.

Most single parents are surprised at how recharged they feel after just a short amount of time spent with caring friends. Even though you may feel you don't have enough time or are afraid you will be judged or pitied, take the risk. It's worth it. Positive friends who share your sense of humor and values can give you a safe place to vent, cry and dream about a better future. Accepting friends will support you, even if you feel ambivalent and are unsure about yourself. Leaning on emotionally supportive adults to meet your needs is a safety net so you don't slip into leaning on your child for support.

Parents who encourage their children to be their emotional support at this challenging time of life are inadvertently stealing their childhoods. Children need to trust and believe their parents are emotionally strong enough to care for them. When a parent shares their deep grief and outbursts of rage at the other parent with their child, the child learns that their parent is unstable and may not be able to protect and support them. Children who are taken into inappropriate confidences of a parent may like the power of being treated like an adult, but will also hide their own strong emotions and challenges from the intense parent as a way of protecting them from any more stress. Conversations about your finances or sex life, or those of the other parent, are inappropriate and harm children.

Sad and frightened divorcing parents do need to talk about money, sex, betrayal, fear, rage, devastation, and confusion. These topics need to be shared with other adults, away from and out of earshot of children. I find that parents think children don't know what they're talking about if they're on the phone and children only hear one side of the conversation. Don't believe this! Children are very intuitive and during times of transition and change, they are extremely curious.

Again, there is nothing you can do about your ex's behavior and their conversations with your child. You can spend time with your child and remind them that they can do things to make themselves feel better, no matter what happens. If your child is complaining that other kids are "making" them feel bad, or believe that they are overly responsible for making other kids happy, these are opportunities for you to explain to your child that everyone is responsible for their own feelings. Be very sure to model this. Don't tell your child, "You made me mad," or "You made me do that," or "Be good and make me proud." Don't vent about other adults and accuse them of making you feel this or that. Model taking responsibility for your own emotional state. Use phrases like: "I feel grumpy. I'm going to sit and read for a bit." "I feel angry. I'm going to go work out." "I feel sad. I'm going to take some alone time. I'll be back in five minutes."

The more time you spend with positive, motivated friends, the less likely you will try to make your child your emotional peer. The more your child watches you handle your feelings, the more likely they'll be to use the skills you model, like talking to friends, writing, listening to music, exercising, being creative, eating healthy, making plans with others, complimenting yourself, using the punching bag in the garage, finding fulfillment in your life's work, etc..

Be careful about what you say around your child. Remember kids are often literal in their thinking. Saying things like "I'm dying to...," "There's not enough money," "I'm going to kill...," are all terrifying things to a child who takes things literally. Speak respectfully to your child and about everyone in your child's life. Don't model hate and retaliation.

No matter how scared or angry you are, share these sentiments with your friends, not your children. Let your child have a childhood, even through difficult times. They deserve that. Keep your focus on your children when they are with you, the attention can be on you when you are with your friends.

If you feel isolated and that you don't have the time or energy to make new friends (or nurture the ones you have) spend time and resources on yourself. Get up a half hour before the kids and sit outside with a cup of tea or coffee. No electronics. Just breathe and be still. If your kids are with your ex part of the time, don't use that free time to just do errands and chores. Spend some of it doing things that rejuvenate you. Doing yoga, running, biking, cooking, baking, playing an instrument, journaling, doing a hobby, volunteering, gardening, scrapbooking, reading, learning a new language or skill, meditating, singing, swimming, or investing resources into that dream you've been neglecting, can all help recharge your batteries when you're not with your child.

If you don't get a built-in break with visitation to their other parent's home, find reliable babysitters. If you spend every moment that you're not sleeping, at work, or doing chores with your child, burnout is likely to happen. With burnout comes an unhealthy reliance on your child that forces them into an emotional role that can have long-term consequences. No matter what happens at the other home, your child should be able to trust that they will be emotionally safe with you. This serenity can make all the difference. It gives your child an emotionally safe place to develop resiliency.

Chapter 11

GIVE YOUR CHILD A VOCABULARY FOR THEIR EMOTIONS

"And then you didn't show up!" Vickie shouted. "You never do what you say!"

"You know that's not true! It was one time, and I couldn't help it. Show some respect!" Her father snapped back. "Don't you ever think about anyone other than yourself?"

Vickie stared out the car window. Dad never listens. He doesn't even care about how I feel!

"Don't you ignore me, young lady!" Her dad looked at her in the rearview mirror.

All he cares about is being right. He never even asks about my feelings. Vicki thought.

"You know you can always tell me how you feel," her dad said. "Right?"

"I do and then you call me a liar," she said, under her breath.

"I heard that," her father said. "And I never called you a liar."

He just did it again, she thought.

They drove toward his house. The air conditioner blew cool air into the back seat. All the divorce books and podcasts he'd listen to swirled through his thoughts. He just wanted to fix this and have his daughter happy with him again. But she exaggerated everything. He had to be the adult here.

"Were you disappointed that time I couldn't come get you?" he asked.

"I just told you that!" Vickie said.

He took a long breath. Don't make her wrong, he said over and over to himself. Just listen for her feelings, not the veracity of her facts.

"You sound annoyed that I didn't understand that," he said.

"Oh, so you can tell." She kept looking out the window. A shiny piece of a torn sticker clung to the glass. The air from the AC whipped her hair into her face. "Genius."

It took all his willpower and his dedication to being the father he'd vowed to be, to keep from snapping back. "When you talk like that, I feel sad and a bit annoyed." He looked up at the mirror again. "I'm glad you can tell me when you feel hurt or angry."

Vickie met his eyes in the mirror. "Doesn't seem like it."

"Yeah, I'm still trying to find the right words for what I want to say, he said. "I'm frustrated that it's so hard."

"And you're the grown up!" She laughed.

He smiled, "I'm the luckiest dad in the world."

72

It's impossible to give children tools to handle their uncomfortable feelings if they have no words to tell you how they're feeling. Most children learn words for abstractions (things they can't touch or see) long after they have mastered a vocabulary for concrete things in their world.

MODEL EXPRESSING FEELINGS AND COPING SKILLS

The best way to teach children anything is through modeling. Labeling your own feelings, "frustrated," "agitated," "tired," "happy," "grateful," "sad," or "annoyed" will give your child an opportunity to use feeling words as well. Be sure not to blame others for those feelings. Everyone is always responsible for their own emotions.

GIVE CHILDREN TOOLS TO EXPRESS THEMSELVES

Read books about divorce together. Help give your child a vocabulary to ask questions and to talk about how they feel. If these words aren't used regularly, children don't know how to talk about the changes that are happening to the family.

Go to an educational supply store or look online for posters with faces and emotions. Post it where your child can see it. In the evening, take turns pointing to and describing feelings you each experienced that day.

Help your child cut out pictures that represent their emotions from magazines and paste them on a poster board. Collages of feelings can help a child identify and label emotional states. Teach your child how to write poetry, lyrics, or short stories. Sculpting with clay or drawing with chalk can help them express how they feel.

Approach talking with children about uncomfortable feelings a little at a time. Set a timer if need be to keep conversations short (5 to 10 min). Use a "talking stick." It can be any small object that indicates whose turn it is to talk. No one can interrupt whoever is holding the talking stick. When they finish, they can give it to another person who also cannot be interrupted so long as they are holding the talking stick.

Stop when your child becomes tired or wants to change activities. Don't pressure them to talk. Remember, the best conversations are going to happen naturally when you are in the middle of some another activity. It's better to listen for opportunities and make the most of them than it is to try to pressure anyone into talking about vulnerable things at a set time.

Find calm ways to discuss this difficult topic. You don't have to arrive at any conclusions. Emotions are experienced. They change. They are each individual's responsibility. It is kind to be present and listen when a child is in emotional pain. It is unkind to try to hurry them through and fix it quickly. Don't try to distract them or give them another way to look at things too quickly. They won't care how mucy you know until they know how much you care.

MODEL COPING WITH FEELINGS

Label your own feelings ("I feel stressed," "This is hard for me," or "I'm getting angry"). Remember, a feeling is not an action. An emotion is an internal state. A behavior is an external action. Say what you're going to do to handle your uncomfortable emotions: "I'm going to go for a walk." "I'm going to read for a bit." Then come back and tell your child you feel better: "Okay, I feel better. Let's talk." "Well, I feel much better! Let's make dinner."

GATHER NEW INFORMATION

Read or listen to books. Listen to podcasts or watch videos on divorce, grief and single parenting. Let your children see that getting new information changes how you speak and react, it changes how you take responsibility for your own feelings, and it changes how you listen to their expression of feelings.

KEEP THE THINGS YOU CAN CHANGE
SEPARATE FROM THE THINGS YOU CAN'T

Don't waste precious energy on things over which you have no control.

Remember you can set up rules and activities in your own household, but you have no control over the other household. Kids raise their hands to speak at school, but know they don't have to at home. Kids are smart. They can adapt to different rules in different environments, as long as the rules are consistent within an environment.

Use words for your emotions:

FEELING WORDS: UNCOMFORTABLE FEELINGS

Sad, Frustrated, Annoyed, Upset, Angry, Irritated, Outraged, Terrified, Afraid, Worried, Apprehensive,

Obsessed, Anxious, Scared, Tired, Overwhelmed, Discouraged, Disappointed, Guilty, Ashamed, Hopeless, Helpless, Grumpy, Agitated, Jealous, Fearful, Gloomy, Depressed, Unhappy, Defeated, Hurt, Resentful, Dubious, Confused, Embarrassed, Humiliated, Defensive, Shocked, Lethargic, Bored, Left Out, Cautious, Vengeful, Invisible, Misunderstood, Confined, Isolated, Distracted, Lost, Baffled, Rushed, Pressured, Miserable, Empty, Exhausted

COMFORTABLE FEELINGS

Grateful, Happy, Joyful, Motivated, Thoughtful, Loving, Curious, Proud, Calm, Excited, Hopeful, Peaceful, Relaxed, Forgiving, Courageous, Brave, Connected, Elated, Rested, Focused, Believing, Resilient, Powerful, Energized, Vulnerable, Humble, Surprised, Pensive, Funny, Lucky, Delighted, Fulfilled, Competent, Valued, Loved, Humorous, Safe, Glad, At Ease, Caring, Justified, Comfortable, Vindicated, Serene, Attractive, Loving, Understood, Free, Relieved, Quiet, Confident, Generous, Motivated, Effective, Satisfied, Energetic

Give yourself credit as you face the changes in your family. The kinder and more complimentary you are of yourself, the more you will have specific words to encourage your children. As you care for yourself and focus on building your own resiliency through adversity, you'll be a role model for your fortunate child. You're on your way to helping your child grow into a strong, resilient, and productive adult.

Resources For Further Reading:

Aron, *The Highly Sensitive Child: Helping Our Children Thrive When the World Overwhelms Them,* Harmony, 2002.

Baker, Amy J.L. and Fine, Paul R. *Co-parenting with a Toxic Ex: What to Do When Your Ex-Spouse Tries to Turn the Kids Against You.* New Harbinger Publications, 2014.

Faber, Adele and Mazlish, Elaine. *How to Talk So Kids Will Listen & Listen So Kids Will Talk.* Scribner, 2012.

Faber, Joanna and King, Julie. *How to Talk so Little Kids Will Listen: A Survival Guide to Life with Children Ages 2-7.* Scribner, 2017.

Kiersey, *Please Understand Me,* Prometheus Nemesis Book Company, 1984.

Wolf, *Get Out of My Life, but First Could You Drive Me and Cheryl to the Mall,* Farrar, Strauss and Giroux, 2002.

Nightingale, Lois. *My Parents Still Love Me Even Though They're Getting Divorced: A healing story and workbook for children.* Nightingale Rose Publications, 2016.

Pedro-Carroll, JoAnne. *Putting Children First: Proven Parenting Strategies for Helping Children Thrive Through Divorce.* Avery, 2010.

Ricci, Isolina. *Mom's House, Dad's House: Making Two Jomes for Your Child.* Touchstone, 1997.

Ross, Julie A. and Corcoran, Judy. *Joint Custody with a Jerk: Raising a Child with an Uncooperative Ex- A Hands-on, Practical Guide to Communicating with a Difficult Ex-Spouse.* St. Martin's Griffin, 2011.

Seligman, *The Optimistic Child: A Proven Program to Safeguard Children Against Depression and Build Lifelong Resilience,* Mariner Books, 2009

89439333R00044

Made in the USA
San Bernardino, CA
25 September 2018